BARRiO

José's Neighborhood

George Ancona

HARCOURT BRACE & COMPANY   *San Diego   New York   London*

Requests for permission to make copies of any part of the work should be mailed to: Permissions Department, Harcourt Brace & Company, 6277 Sea Harbor Drive, Orlando, Florida 32887-6777.

The author would like to acknowledge the muralists whose work brightens José's neighborhood and the pages of this book: "Silent Language of the Soul/El lenguaje mudo del alma" copyright © 1990 Juana Alicia and Susan Kelk Cervantes; all rights reserved. "Si se puede" copyright © 1995 Juana Alicia, Margo Bors, Susan Kelk Cervantes, Gabriela Lujan, Olivia Quevedo, and Elba Rivera; all rights reserved. "500 Years of Resistance" copyright © 1993 Isaías Mata; all rights reserved. "Maestrapeace" copyright © 1994 Juana Alicia, Miranda Bergman, Edythe Boone, Susan Kelk Cervantes, Meera Desai, Yvonne Littleton, and Irene Pérez; all rights reserved. "Culture Continued: The Seed of Resistance Which Blossoms into the Flower of Liberation" copyright © 1984 Miranda Bergman and O'Brien Thiele; all rights reserved.

Library of Congress Cataloging-in-Publication Data
Ancona, George.
Barrio: José's neighborhood/George Ancona.
p.   cm.
Summary: Presents life in a barrio in San Francisco, describing the school, recreation, holidays, and family life of an eight-year-old boy who lives there.
ISBN 0-15-201049-1   ISBN 0-15-201048-3   *(pb)*
1. Mexican American families—California—San Francisco—Social life and customs—Juvenile literature.   2. Mission District (San Francisco, Calif.)—Social life and customs—Juvenile literature.   3. San Francisco (Calif.)—Social life and customs—Juvenile literature.   [1. Mexican Americans—San Francisco (Calif.)   2. San Francisco (Calif.)—Social life and customs.]   I. Title.
F869.S39M53   1998
979.4'610046872073—dc21   97-29667

Title hand-lettered by Pablo Ancona
Text set in Galliard
Designed by George Ancona and Camilla Filancia

First edition
L K J I H G F E D C   L K J I H G F   (pb)

Printed in Singapore

Gracias. My thanks go out to the people who helped make this book possible. To José Luís Ferreira Jr. and his family, who welcomed me into their lives. To Pilar Mejía, the principal of the Cesar Chavez Elementary School, and to Rebecca García-Gonzalez, Francisco Javier Herrera, Betty Pazmiño, Marta Estrella, the teachers who invited me into their classrooms. To the principal, Adelina Arámbola, and to the teachers and parents of the Buena Vista Elementary School, who permitted me to photograph their exuberant celebration of *Carnaval*. To Felipe Pasmanick, for allowing me to reproduce his song, "Birds Have No Borders." To María Pinedo, Mía Gonzalez, and Gloria Jaramillo of Galería de la Raza, for their encouragement, help, and hospitality during my visits to the barrio. To Susan Cervantes, Juana Alicia, Olivia Quevedo, and Inti Guzmán, of the Precita Eyes Mural Arts Center, for allowing me to look over their shoulders while they worked. To Isaís Mata, who let me photograph his mural on the rectory walls of St. Peter's Church. And to all the people whose smiles and answers to my questions made me feel welcomed in their barrio.

THE MISSION DISTRICT of San Francisco got its name from the Mission Dolores. Built by Spanish missionaries, the church was completed in 1791 and is the oldest building in San Francisco. The district has always been home to many immigrants from Europe, Asia, and Latin America who came to settle in Northern California. But since the Second World War, the majority of the neighborhood's immigrants have come from Mexico and other countries south of the U.S. border, and the district has taken on a distinctive Latino flavor.

In this small corner of the United States, one can see how the country's new residents remake their lives while preserving the culture they've come from. The people here affectionately call the Mission District *El barrio*.

José Luís lives in the barrio and goes to the Cesar Chavez Elementary School. He and his family speak only Spanish at home, but at school he is in a Spanish-English bilingual class. The school reflects the diverse needs and interests of the barrio, and in addition to Spanish also offers Chinese bilingual classes and a black history program.

José's teacher, Señora Rebecca, talks to him about his homework before sending him out for recess. When asked what he likes about school, José says, "I like my teacher, drawing, and sports." He grins. "But not homework."

Like kids everywhere, José and his schoolmates climb the jungle gym and play games during recess. A favorite game is cops and robbers. The cops count *one, two, three, four…* as the robbers hide around the school yard. On *twenty,* the cops shout, "*CÓRRELE!*" and run to find and arrest the robbers. Each robber must wait "in jail" on a bench until all his teammates are rounded up. If a "free" robber can get to the bench, he can release the kids on his side so that the cops have to round up the robbers all over again. When all the robbers are captured, everyone switches sides.

On the back of the school, a new mural is being painted. The central figure is Cesar Chavez, the Mexican American man who led the long and bitter nonviolent struggle to organize the United Farm Workers Union. When he died, in 1993, teachers and parents named the school after him. The mural is the work of artists who have also painted many other buildings in the barrio.

The murals of the barrio sing out the stories of the neighborhood. A portrait of Rigoberta Menchú dominates one side of the Women's Building. She spoke out against the killing of her people, the Maya of Guatemala, and was awarded the Nobel Peace Prize in 1993.

José looks up at the murals on the St. Peter's Church rectory. They were painted by an artist from El Salvador who had been a political prisoner in his country. The church managed to get him out of El Salvador by inviting him to San Francisco to paint the rectory. The mural depicts some of the native cultures of the Americas, and honors their men and women who struggled for social justice.

Because of the murals, a walk through the barrio is like a walk through the history of the people who live here. Very often, immigrants living in the barrio are refugees who fled their countries to save their lives. Many have seen friends and relatives killed, and decided to seek safety in the United States. Others have come to escape poverty. Some are so desperate that they are here without proper permits. This means they have no legal right to work in this country, and so often are paid very little for their work.

Some immigrants return to their homelands when life there gets better. Others find it difficult to return once their children have grown up in the United States. Members of many families stay and become citizens, as did the immigrants who founded this country. These new immigrants believe that if they work hard their children will have a better life.

Carnaval is the biggest fiesta in the barrio and is celebrated in the spring. It brings together the people of the barrio for a weekend of music, dance, and a parade.

For weeks the children of the Buena Vista Elementary School have been rehearsing for *Carnaval*. They are using birds as a symbol of freedom because birds recognize no borders. Parents, teachers, and students build a float in the shape of a giant bird, complete with flapping wings.

On Sunday everyone joins the parade. The students and teachers wear bird costumes with wings and feathers. On the float they sing a bilingual call-and-response song written by one of their teachers:

Birds have no borders
    We take no orders
You don't know
    We do so
Voy por doquiera
    No hay frontera
¿Y tú qué sabes?
    Somo aves

*I go anywhere / There is no border / What do you know? / We are birds

Children from barrio schools and people of many cultures march in the parade. The marchers wave flags to the rhythms of salsa, reggae, merengue, and samba. Towering stilt walkers dance in the streets with masked, costumed revelers. Marchers in wheelchairs are followed by skaters on Rollerblades. A clown juggles while another plays his trombone to the cheering spectators on the sidewalks.

One street is closed to traffic for several blocks, and food stands, rides, and two stages have been set up. The delicious smells of tacos, barbecue, dumplings, gyros, and many other dishes from around the world fill the air. Musicians on stages at either end of the street play music throughout the weekend.

Besides fiestas, other activities bring neighbors together. Three community gardens in the barrio keep people busy during the summer months. One borders a new playground where neighbors plant shrubbery. In another garden, parents and children plant seeds and harvest vegetables in their own individual garden plots.

Many of the houses in the barrio are very old. Some have beautifully carved doors and archways and window moldings, and are painted in bright colors. José Luís lives in one of these houses with his parents and sisters, Susy and little Fabiola.

José Luís's parents came to this country when they were teenagers. His father came here to study and met José Luís's mother. They married and moved into an apartment that a relative offered them.

Nearly all of José's family lives nearby. Only his grandfather and one aunt still live in Mexico. In the summers, José visits them and gets to ride horses.

But the barrio isn't perfect. José doesn't like the *pandillas*, the street gangs. And he doesn't like the drunks who sit around drinking and smoking on the playgrounds. But despite the problems, José's parents don't plan to move from the barrio. They point out that every neighborhood has its problems. And besides, as his father says, they're "too busy watching our children growing up."

Soccer is the most popular sport in the barrio. José has been playing with his neighborhood team for five years. He has won many trophies. On Saturday José's father takes him to play a match in another neighborhood. During the game his father calls out advice to José from the sidelines. José makes two goals and his team wins 3–1. Tomorrow José will watch his dad play with a grown-up team.

CARNICERIA
BIRRIA
MENUDO
CARNITAS
CHICHARRONES
TACOS
Burritos
MEAT
LIQUOR
GROCERIE
CATESSE

Twenty-fourth street is one of the main avenues of the barrio, where many stores sell imported foods from Latin America. Signs along the street are in Spanish, English, and sometimes a mixture of both. *Taquerías*, *carnicerías*, *boticas*, *panaderías*, and *mexicatessens* line both sides of the street. José accompanies his mother and baby sister, Fabiola, when they go shopping. They buy *jitomates*,*nopales*, *plátanos machos*, mangoes, and mole. José pays. His father wants José to know the value of money and what it can buy.

Down the street, they turn into the *panadería*, where the smells of cinnamon and vanilla fill the store. They buy *pan dulce*. It is hard for José to choose which of the tasty, sugar-coated buns to buy for tomorrow's breakfast. The last stop of the day is for an ice-cream cone, which José shares with Fabiola.

Fall brings Halloween, a time for masks, witches, pumpkins, and fun. At Cesar Chavez Elementary, a parade is held in the school yard. Each class is led by a costumed teacher. The principal, Pilar Mejía, is a good fairy who taps José and other students with her magic wand.

A father entertains everyone with a juggling-and-comedy act. The children giggle and watch in awe.

After Halloween the barrio prepares for November 2, *El día de los muertos,* the Day of the Dead, a festive holiday in which the living remember the dear departed. Children make skull masks. Candy makers turn out hundreds of sugar skulls, which they decorate and adorn with children's names. The skulls are given as gifts, along with tasty *pan de muertos,* bread of the dead.

Comical papier-mâché skeletons dressed in everyday clothes are hung everywhere to make fun of the living and of death itself. Not even the baker's deliveryman or the candy maker is spared.

Along the streets, storekeepers put *ofrendas*, offerings, in their windows to honor dead relatives and friends. At Cesar Chavez Elementary, an altar is set up in the lobby so that students and teachers will have a place to display pictures of dead loved ones. Among the photographs is a picture of a favorite teacher who died of AIDS. Pictures, drawings, food, and toys are placed on the altar as offerings. At home José lights a candle in memory of his grandparents.

The students and teachers go to the
Golden Gate AIDS Memorial Grove
to honor the memory of their teacher
who died the year before. They sing
songs, and then Brother Mfuasi, a
teacher, offers a libation, a ceremony
of pouring water on the earth.
Another teacher helps the children
perform the Asian ceremony of
burning letters written to the
deceased. The children's thoughts
become smoke that floats up to their
beloved teacher.

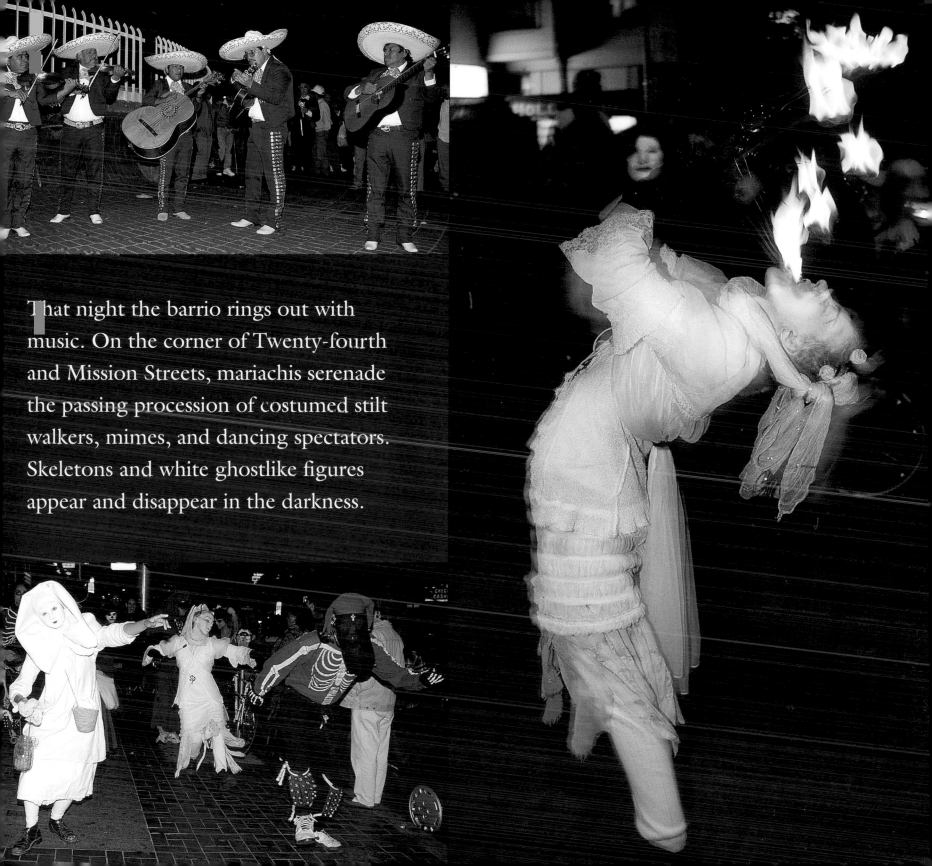

That night the barrio rings out with music. On the corner of Twenty-fourth and Mission Streets, mariachis serenade the passing procession of costumed stilt walkers, mimes, and dancing spectators. Skeletons and white ghostlike figures appear and disappear in the darkness.

A few months later, when
José's birthday approaches, he
and his mother go shopping
for a piñata from Mexico. He
cranes his neck to look at the
many different piñatas hanging
from the ceiling. José finally
decides on a horse and carries
it home on his head.

In the kitchen, his mother cooks turkey with mole sauce, rice, and tortillas, and helps José fill the piñata with candy for him and his friends.

When José's father gets home from work, he ties the filled piñata to a rope. Then he climbs up on a ladder and dangles the piñata above the head of the first blind-folded batter. Unfortunately, the first blow knocks off the horse's head. "They don't make these piñatas like they used to," says José's dad as he tapes the piñata together for the other children to hit. Finally the piñata bursts and all the children leap to gather handfuls of the scattered candy.

Afterward the boys immediately start a basketball game using a milk crate with its bottom knocked out as a basket. But the game is cut short as José's mother calls down from the back stairs that dinner is ready.

The children sit down to plates laden with turkey legs, rice, and mole sauce. Everyone takes some hot jalapeño peppers from a bowl in the middle of the table. José's mother keeps the tortillas coming from the stove. She sits down to eat only after everyone else has finished. Then José's father passes *her* the warm tortillas.

José's older sister, Susy, helps her mother clear the dishes. Now everyone gathers for the cutting of the cake. While José stands beaming behind the cake, they sing "*Cumpleaños feliz*" to the traditional tune of "Happy Birthday."

José blows out the candles and everyone begins to shout, *"¡Que lo muerda! ¡Que lo muerda!"* ("Bite it! Bite it!")

As José leans over to bite the cake, one of his cousins pushes his face into it. José lifts his head and shows off his icing-covered face. Everyone laughs.

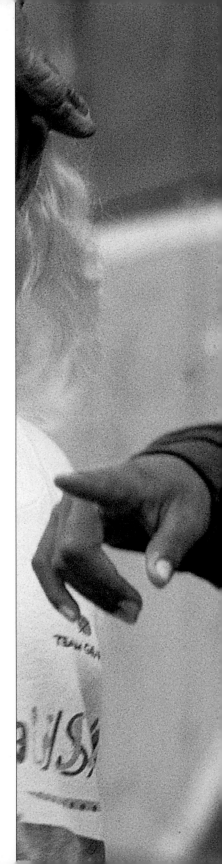

And so José Luís celebrates another birthday in the barrio with his family and friends. Living in the barrio makes it easy for him to keep many of the customs and traditions of his parents while he also learns about the different cultures of his classmates and the people in his neighborhood. For José, the barrio is more than his home—it is a window that opens onto the entire world.

Some Words Used in the Barrio

barrio	a neighborhood
botica	a drugstore or pharmacy
Carnaval	a springtime festival before Lent
carnicería	a butcher's shop or meat market
compleaños felíz	happy birthday
¡Córrele!	Run!
El día de los muertos	The Day of the Dead, a holiday
fiesta	a party or celebration
gracias	thank you
Guatemala	a country in Central America
jalapeño	a variety of hot pepper
jitomate	a variety of tomato
mango	a tropical fruit
merengue	a dance from the Dominican Republic
mexicatessen	a store selling a variety of prepared Latin foods
mole	a sauce made with chile, chocolate, and spices
nopal	a prickly pear cactus
ofrenda	an offering
panadería	a bakery
pan de muertos	bread of the dead
pandilla	a street gang
pan dulce	sweet bread
piñata	decorated hanging pot or container filled with candy
plátano macho	plantain, a banana used for cooking
reggae	a Jamaican music that blends calypso, blues, and rock and roll
salsa	a sauce, also a Latin dance rhythm
El Salvador	a country in Central America
samba	a dance rhythm from Brazil
taquería	a taco stand or restaurant
tortilla	a thin, round, flat Mexican bread